Always Messing with them Boys

D0851759

Always Messing with them Boys

Jessica Helen Lopez

West End Press
2011

Some of these poems have been published in *Adobe Walls, A Bigger Boat, Destructable Heart Press's Family Album, Duke City Fix-Sunday Poem, New Mecca Earthships, The Pedestal,* and *Venus Envy,*

Some of these poems have been recorded for the following CD anthologies – *Strength Vibrations, Ordinary Woman,* and *Green Chile Stew: Only in New Mexico.*

Always Messing with them Boys © 2011 by Jessica Helen Lopez
Printed in the United States of America

No part of this book may be performed, recorded, or otherwise transmitted without the written consent of the author and the permission of the publisher. However, portions of the poems may be cited for book reviews without gaining such consent.

First Print Edition May 2011
ISBN: 978-0-9826968-4-2

Front and back cover photographs by Gina Marselle.
Book design by Bryce Milligan.

West End Press
P.O. Box 27334
Albuquerque, NM 87125

For book information, see our web site at
www.westendpress.org

Contents

*These poems and all my love
are dedicated to my daughter,
Mia "Sopapilla" Rivera*

Always Messing with them Boys

Mama

Mama is a boozehound
she'll spit poetry
and bourbon fire from her throat
sheave your heart in a clean split
of mean tongue and a bottle of bad emotions
she'll dethrone what you thought was yours
Molotov your insides like a top-shelf
margarita on the rocks
care little if she spills
down the cleavage of her blouse
a carnival makeshift make-up mouth
spitting wet kisses and
beer-heavy breath
painted lips in
stop sign red
sloppy from the third round

Mama is a pretty lady
sewed up smile
quaint like a rag-time doll
red and bow-like for public
appearances,
mirrors

Mama is a depressed bird
gilded-caged tongue
a ball and chain suffocates
her meaning of life and freedom
plucks at her parrot-plume of poem
bald and ashamed
at the thought that words
ever needed living for
dying for
wishing she felt that way
about her babies

her old man
prose just another
bad habit
praise too addictive

Oh, Sagrado Corazon de Maria!
Oh, Sagrado Corazon de Jesus!

If only I was a praying woman,
ate up the hope for a savior
like a communion wafer
melting beneath the tongue
on another hopeless Sunday
If only I could bleed at the feet, too
like my mother
the martyr
like all mothers are meant to be
heads laid out in a gas stove
while thoughts of sugar plums
dance in the dreams
of children
in the next room

because I
don't pray
I live,

Mama
is a boozehound and I paint
my eyes to look just like hers

Palomas en la Frontera

We wore our coats beautifully,
glistening in red velveteen
that shimmered like blood.
In the right kind of sunlight,
our razor blade eyebrows
arched magnificent like
black crayon sickles

Stenciled hair like a gateway
to heaven above our eyes
an archway
If you dare
into our gaze,

but when the night fell,
casting her shawl across
our small border town
young bodies press into
the sides of a car
any car

leave behind the
thumbprint of our desire
our anger like smoldering charcoal
the shame of our fathers.

Flames licked at our shadows
as our virginity slipped through our fingers
stark images of our female selves
cut against a milieu of
masculine lowriders
parked around the circle of fire

We didn't imagine us
as young mothers one day
men we did not or did love caressed
our eager ears with their shrapnel tongues

To fuck or fight our way
into the desert air,
bulge against a backdrop
of cactus and dried mesquite

The legend of the Chola
see her there, dancing in the moonlight,
arms embracing the lunar verbosity
ferocity gleaning the carnal smile
and Mad Dog 20/20 breath
existing only in cliché

But we were something
harder than that, rocks
without smooth edges
belt buckles,
brothers emptied
of their blood in a manic drive-by,
our mothers in their aprons
slapping our behinds
with wooden spoons
like crucifixes
beating the devil
from us.

Our near future
the long lines we will
wait in to gain the coveted
commodities of cheese
and powdered milk

The part of our brains
that recognize such incidents
make us the lovers we are
even me, in my diluted ways,
book pages swirling in my head
no type of academic rant
could beat this night
this night with arms like brute
strength and prison tattoos

Hold me, held me,
made me one with my girls
convinced me of violence
beautiful, slow moving violence
that somehow by the end
of the night makes babies,
fabricates love
in the backseats of cars
cries out into the air
a cumbia riddled with
spur and cacti,
a red fist

We are bent on destroying ourselves
I am bent on destroying myself

The open eye of the moon and the burn of tire
black smoke shredding the night
ritmo inspired legends
lead me to believe I could love like this
love like I carried a razor blade in my back pocket

Here no one gave one good goddamn
that my name was inked across some college degree
that I could recite all of Frost's poems in a single breath
dissertations have no dominion here

So, I fall back with the mob
sashay my hips and dance
with Manny at the local saloon
two-step with young drunk
ranchers named Bud or Shay or Cliff
make my way easy with tequila
at two-dollars a pop
a squinty eyed piece of lime
squeezed down my throat
and don't think
nothing of no professors

Tonight,
I shove back into me my home
I once rebuked
for lettermen jackets and scrolled diplomas

Choke me in memory
strangle the moon
until I cough up
the dry sweet granules
of desert and the salty sky
that rims my glass

Until I see, see
see my way
back to me.

don de dios

There's a scorpion in the soup
a serpent in the house
a spider that sleeps between the sheets
There's a barefoot bruja who despises shoes
and walks about in chanclas beneath a winter moon
in her heart there is a ballad that hums a tune
sings a song sinew
a *sinverguenza curandera*
shucking archetypes
shunning the discrete
mumbling prayers and deflecting curses
she cohorts at the crux of crosses
cleaning out the soul with a whisk broom
conjuring the early
morning
diaphanous
moon
the pregnant swoon of femininity
for the wont of wombs
and longing loins
she's cooking up curanderismo in the kitchen
covering the mirrors with cloth
shaking hands with the *mano peluda*
making love to the *lechuza*
spirit hostess owl
yerba buena warms her guests
befriends
she offers them benediction
protects them with the oval of an egg
to ward away the ominous ojo
she hikes her skirt in the sand
and births her babies in the motherland

like her abuelita
and her abuelita
before that
when the Watermelon Mountain
was still *Mejico*
still Indigo
when indigenous tongues lapped the lands
before the Christians
before the Dukes

a baptismal by fire
that rebuked her religion
healed her with holy water
made her heavy with Jesus
so she took to the book
shook up the bible
molded her own Magdalena
gave the Guadalupe her rightful place
and claimed the crucifix in the name of Aztlan
the crucible of her convictions
the song of her land

Dangerous Woman

I've got no qualms
on being a woman
no problem with my
swinging hips, paint my lips
a Nefertiti type of chick
a fret-none, foul-mouthed
drink some beer kind of bitch
laugh with the girls
smoldering cigarillo
hangs on hard lips

I'm a quick-wit pessimist
born with a bad disposition
bonding bartenders and
waitress sisterhood
up to no good

that dangerous table
back of the bar shadows
black widows chewing
up men throwing
back beers
half-cocked
cocked rifle
my poem
a revolution
on the horizon

tipsy chatter
shackle-free
of mean daddies
fast-fisted husbands
seventy-cents on the dollar

double standards and
sorry ass sexual innuendoes
scratching where I please
another round of brew, please
remove your hands
from my ass,
please
a tease
stomping through life
squeezed into lean jeans

I'm a contradiction
wearing a barely-there-bra,
bulldozing bullshit,
those that aim
to hurt me
those that aren't
not knowing
any difference
a hangover of regrets
and smudged mascara

what to do with
this anger
like a man?

this tongue
like a proprietor
of porn?

where do I fit
between dainty decent
and vulgar truth?

saintly and slutty?
maternal and murderous?

Butt –
of a cigarette
a beautiful thing
sexy beer bottle
and smoking Marlboro Lights
down to the last stick
last match
last call

I've got no qualms
with alcohol
smooth and fluid
ten-feet-tall
heavy-handed eye
shadow hooded lids
sling my arrows aim
to miss

swinging hips
painted lips
dangerous
woman

Pre-Pubescent Ruminations from a Tree

I wanted more than dust-speckled dreams and a Daddy who hollered red-spotted commands through a summer-screen door. That time of day, the afternoon brought about only contempt for man-made time. The sun hung from a noose above our heads and I counted minutes like years. Even our dogs draped their furrowed brows low in defeat.

I was hoping for some type of happiness that might roll in on the back of a southern breeze or the slow strut of a Tex-Mex *caballero*, a border dwelling ranch hand who could dip his tongue into a sweet batch of Spanglish just for me. He would be a romance telenovela in the flesh, one that I couldn't comprehend because I never did speak Spanish anyways. Nonetheless, my *caballero* would roll a cinnamon-flavored toothpick between a pair of purple-scented Mestizo lips, a fatter cigarillo between his fingers.

I spent those summer days chewing on dusty piñon shells and wondering what another tongue in my mouth might taste like. I spat the shells to the ground and they glistened with my saliva. I spent the idle hours cradled by the branches of my front-yard tree reading about sex in slow whispers and the grind of bark against the back of my thighs. The v-cut shape of a book embedded into the skin, right where my jeans met in the middle of me and me and into me.

Had my father ever known the types of thoughts I had slinking about my adolescent brain, he would have cut my very legs so that I may never have left the yard. He would have rattle-chained me to the fence and shorn my hair like a boy. He would have tamed my fire tongue of heat and flame and root by plucking it out and burying it in the backyard. He would have taken the blood for himself if he could've.

If he could have.

Or at least that's how I always figured it.

You could tell me otherwise, but I wouldn't believe you.

Always Messing with them Boys

The night permeates like a blood orchid
bursting with the smell of wet caliche
through my open bedroom window.

One lamp is lit, the color of dusk.
Curled like a fist around my cigarette,
I am stuck in the knuckle of my thoughts.

Late nights like this urge me to push out a poem.
A fat candle burns at three wicks,
the scent of midnight pomegranates.
It is anything but red in here.

In my cotton panties,
I sit and sweat into the pillow,
hair wet down my backbone,
slick as a knife.

Motionless, still I do not
pick up my pen instead, I pinch
out the memory of one afternoon
I kicked ball with the boys,
before the blood came.

My scissor legs were
ashy as the rest,
my scabs half-eaten.

Our eager yells bounced
from the black-top into
the sun-baked air and the trees
splintered the sunlight like long fingers
against my sweaty forehead.

Inside the darkness of our house,
my father sits, a television blinks
like a blue Cyclops and pours
static into his ear.

He is a chunk of meat
frozen to his chair and
Mama is somewhere else

I kicked that ball all day
long as if it were the last
time I would ever kick a ball,
arms cinnamon-dark,
body fast, stealth
like a wet seal slipping in
and around the grasp of
all them boys.

And when the sun boiled
its last cough over our neighborhood
the street lamps burst like marigolds
brilliant bright light
against a grey canopy

Daddy hollered at me,
Come in, stop messing
With them boys
and the screen door
slammed behind me like
a swat across my bottom.

Before the blood came
and there were pomegranates
in my dreams, a purple fist-
shaped bruise beneath my left eye,
a bowl full of stars, a gift
from Daddy as I slept
in my bed.

Mama offered up her finest
eye shadow so both sides of
my face would match,

Ain't you pretty, Mama said
Ain't you?

But, no I never wrote *that*.
Some poems are best left
To rattle inside the head

Like the time she burst
from me as a seed does
With a pair of wilted
flowers for hands
I held her, an empty
husk pressed against
the sterile hospital sheets.

Her eyes stretched
from temple to temple and as
the blood still ran down my thighs
in shooting star color
I wondered if all mothers
are meant to be martyrs

Like when I broke all
the glassware in the house,
bits of porcelain clung to
his hair like snow.
The night I ran her Daddy off,
I swear to you, all those razor
blades winked at me from the
lopsided face of my medicine cabinet.

Always messing with them boys,
pushing the tongue against the teeth

running fingers across a three-wick flame,
always never writing down my poetry

Like this one
still clinging
to the inside of my head,
like clean white linen,
Mama's laundry
and the idea of love

Hey, Bukowski!

Hey, Bukowski!
You boozing hound,
poetic misfit muse!

Hey, pockmarked man!
Big nose and gin blossoms
like my grandfather.
How did you find
your way
into my car?

I have searched these lonely highways
beneath the lunatic smile of
a checkered moon,
by the light of a desert star
awash in the soft glow
of car radio,

For you, Hank!

fat-gutted and beer swollen
splayed crotch riding
the bucket seat of my jeep.

The pessimist is at the wheel again.

We cackle like roosters
spitting into the wind,
my long black hair a flag
whipping the salt from our eyes.

Transgressions like so many
trinkets rattle our pockets.

We are crazy drunk and reckless with poetry
giving no thought to the check stop
just beyond the sloppy road's bend.

What do you think of that, Buk?

May I split
a cigarette
with you?
Put my head
in your lap?
My ugly lover
who fights and fucks
like a boar.

We will select the finest
of ugliest whores,
bet on the lamest
of horses.

Indulge me if you will,
Mr. Chinasky. The rants
of a victim
are the saddest
of all.

Custody

At the restaurant, across the table
of neutral salt shakers and violent forks
our stiff backs like wooden chairs
betray an ancient battle.

We discuss the finer points of divorce
over spilled merlot and plates of cold food.

You speak, and I grit my ears. My face a closed envelope.
I draw lines in the spilt salt with my steak knife.

Our daughter is a dividend
carved from my hip
and a piece of your rib.
She scribbles furious
red circles marking the paper,
bleeding the tablecloth.

Her voiceless soul rustles,
a thousand shards of glittering mirrors
hanging like leaves from a tree.

Poised above her delicate head,
her seashell ears, her round face,
hair like fine spun silk,
Solomon's hefty sword ready to burst her
bone from flesh
cut her in half,
one piece for me
one for you.

We swallow the last
of our bitter wine,
split the bill
and part ways.

Red Is the Color of Regret

In the absolute silence
of a midnight house
I paint my toenails red
the color of matador
fanning outward and bleeding
seeping its way across the ridged nail
the askew pinky toe
the soft pulp of cuticle

the red of it frightens me
cocking my head I turn
a constant ear to stairwell
upstairs my infant sleeps

comfort found in still
air and quiet child,
my eyes snap back
hawk like precise
I peck again at my feathers
fawning, preening
for no one

like the quiet flush of red paint
slashed across the Braille of my feet
you flash bright, a sudden
anguish of the arteries
the vacant halls inside my chest
thud suddenly with your clumsy footsteps

you kick over a lamp
with heavy boot
stumble your way into the inside
of the inside of me
nudge the gap between my sternum

you crack open my breastplate
poke around with a capricious thumb
the astuteness of a poet
the sterility of a surgeon
the unwavering ferocity of a star-like lover
fucking our way across the murky linen
of my sleigh-shaped bed

my toes are painted spectacular,
lacquered red and pristine
I hang them out to dry
fan them

admire their ambulance-wail hue
a song you will never hear

for you have zippered your suitcase
buttoned your trousers
spent all the time allowable
a hitchhiker can spare
writing your poem

I am your dusty rumination
a Mona Lisa muse forgotten
accents of red begonia
cupping my ear
scenting my hair

I live here
a sleeping baby breathes
upstairs in our midnight house
colored quiet

an antiquity of still life
sepia misplaced postcard
aged and water-damaged
trapped in the back pocket of
your vagabond blue jeans

dusty

red snapdragons
dot our windowsill
wave in the breeze

Hate Poem

Love had me baying at the hot moon like a fool dog
a mad bitch, set aflame by her own rabid stupidity,
crooning a torch song and dancing on my own grave

I watered the weeds that crowded my tombstone,
my plot of dirt and worms laid out for the wistful-hearted
tended to my blanket of soil and sorrow
laid it out over my head and played dead

I thought you might attend my funeral –
but you had better things to do
sketch the skyline
trace her curves
with your pencil and charcoal
shade in her throat of dusk and cloud
roll around with her in your white
sheets of of onion-veined paper

Love had me asking why the blues
had to go and pick me
why I had to remember
with crystalline clarity
the honey thumbprints
you left on my thighs
the lines you fed me
dripping of amber and cyanide

the wicked, wicked ways
we plundered my bed
waged war
made love

Love had me not recognizing
my own reflection
rubbed my knees raw
laid me out rigormortis-style
looking like a mad-eyed mascara
witch woman
swollen in her bones
pacing my carpet
leaving it bald with wear
the same silly steps
from bedroom to window
from here to there

Head pressed against the double-
pane sheets of glass
steamed with my heavy breath
my empty breasts
my sagging robe
my silent phone

Love left me a childless mother
a thrill seeker, a junkie
hungry for nothing

Love left me a spoiled child
a tantrum flailing in my gut
a rotten tooth in the back of my mouth
a closet with a coat swinging from a skinny hanger
love left me lonely drunken trumpet player
when the jazz band has called it a night

love left me with a poem I don't want

love left me *flaca*, a dancing skeleton
the grimace of *calavera*
made me a gaggle of bones
singing the bittersweet blues
into a bottle of booze

it left behind bright colors
and migraines, a taste
for martyrdom
sirens and whistles
and a crown of thorns

stitched my spine
to the empty pocket
of my heart
love nailed me
to the cross

split my wrists
love left me aching
like an idiot

love left me spitting
cursing
cussing

love left me chanting
howling
moaning

love left me
love had me
and I hope
that bitch
rots in hell

The Acquiescence of Magdalena and the Rise of Jesus

I wonder if this
is a temporary resurrection
telltale of the leftover
warmed over rosary beads
a forgotten Gnostic priest

he is last night's lover
the semen encrusted cold thighs
against the sinless white sheets
of a carpenter's bed

he is a renaissance risen only
to be forgotten like the
fallen phallic temple that
once placed the promise
of redemption on the
tip of my tongue

The last blush of wine
I grow numb with
the blood of lamb
I have become
tipsy with religion

Romance me
iconoclastic statue
I kiss the cold marble
toes of man
contemplate idyll
hands folded in prayer
and the edifice of you

You
sweaty knees and stiff
starch of the collar
clean sweet priests powdered
in their hallowed halls
making like saints
like gods
like men

and me just a woman
a dark robed nun in the
stomach of monastery and
its tongue tied halls

Bathe me
isolate me
be my father
eclipse my small island
with your communion
wafer moon
blind me with bliss
ignorance like so many
cheap prints of
motel bibles
middle-of-the-night
out of town saviors

The whores of Babel
create you God
I will take your stones
fold them into my
robes of womanly skin
for now

This is the epicenter
of my feebleness

I wonder at my drunkenness
my fall to foolishness

I am ripe for religion
I am whore and mother
you have risen
I let you call me sinner
and you have carved
your name into my flesh
laid our your instruments
of passion and wood
built upon woman

The bonds and fired
bricks of religion
the crucifixion of wife
the acquiescence of me

That Following Sunday

The carpeted halls of the church
sigh and moan under the weight
of my sex, the musk of wax
and wails from beneath veiled hats

The pews complain and hold
back the pantyhose women,
pressed perms and palms
their prayers play to beg
a god to forgive such thoughts

The skin beneath the clothes
stowed away to smother the
heat between the legs under
the mounds of Sunday's best
rippled silk, heavy hosiery and
the crushed kerchief

I avert my eyes
in the holiest of angles
position my gaze to
seem chaste
the thick velvet
tapestries breathe
as I fall to thoughts
of Eve

While my mother mumbles like
the Madonna, she shoulders me
into the corner pew, bullies me
to my knees makes me
heavy with Jesus
as she loses herself to the coupling
of faith she prays for my salvation

The candles sweat
we eat bread
as I remember
like a lost wallet, a forgotten slipper
my virginity remains
in the tangle of sheets
the folds of duvet
and the twist of sex
pillowcases bloodied
by the scarlet letter of
my favorite lipstick
long black hair
coiled on his lumpy mattress
we burned incense and
it smelled like Sunday

And that sordid bible
the dubious note –
that sordid bible!
thick and black and
gilded golden pages
it lay like an empty canoe
on his nightstand
when he undid
my nightshirt
and I let him
and I helped him
that empty eye
socket that stared
the one that taught
me all the sins
I ever needed to know
for many lifetimes over
and over
and over

naked truth
the oddity of beauty
that up-close and
stolen look
small and shriveled
in a heap of hair
the apple of the buttock
the fermented fruit that I invited
to create the gorge
that became the thigh

And I
cross myself
hope to know
we can't all be Mary
and I regret nothing

A Note from Lima
(Monday Mornings, Postcards and Assorted
Piñon and Starlike References)

Like the insides of piñon
the startled meaty fruit of nutseed
caught between the teeth and by surprise
the seed like star pops from its boat of skin
to roll around on the tongue
the shell discarded
left to melt back into the earth

that was me when
I received your postcard
tattooed in exotic postage
and dressed in your eager
penmanship and ballpoint poetry
across wind-swept continents and
the expanse of time

your postcard slept inside the iron
gut of my morning mailbox
its long scribbled arms waiting to wrap
their memories around my neck
all the way from Cusco
all the way from Lima

I popped open from the sleep of my skin
I allowed your words to roll around the tongue
caught between happiness and melancholy
I read and re-read your note from Peru

The individual letters mapped out your travels
spelled out your future plans
the constellation of your heavenly body

tiny crammed script let me
know you
thought of me
crooked little letters spilling
from the tattered corners
falling off the edge of earth
into the mouth of ocean

lingering, I savored the juicy meat
the fruit of your words
the brightly-skinned postcard

startled by the sudden
shooting star of tears
that fell like a light rain
from my naked cheek

I turned my back
then and walked into the wind
back to the warm spot of my apartment
to sip my hot coffee and brush out
my tangled morning hair
like the piñon shell
earthy and dusty
falling from the pine tree
I melted back into the earth

An Offering to the Lover Who Will Leave
for Mexico City
(Five Movements in a Matter of Weeks)

I.

I took you as a lover
bore you like a child
I bit the leather between the teeth
grit my thighs together and squeezed you from me

like Athena
stomached from the head of Zeus
I cleaved you from my skull

you repaid me

sly smiles lit from boyish charm and free spirit
such a young winged-thing, you!

the leather bracelets that hug your wrists
is what did me in
that and how you took your whiskey

silver rings wrapped around the thick fingers
of your flighty pianist hands
my gaze leapt from your face to the vibrancy of those hands

you were too soon.

I gazed with a jealous eye
let you go before I owned you
knowing that I could destroy you

these, my bevy of bad habits.

I pitied myself then and hid my face
the benign Medusa

the Mercurial Me
the sleepy housewife

I have not yet molted.
you were too good to me
my heart much too heavy and Atlas
himself could not grunt this work

your feet were swift as you trampled about the globe
I wondered at you and ate your stories of world
women and decadence
free will to gaze upon Picasso, Goya, Kahlo

breezily you walked the halls of Rome
paid a philosophical visit to Caesar and ate your sandwiches
beneath the long shadow of the Sistine
popped an olive into your mouth

II.

sip wine at high noon for me
feel every smooth groove of the centuries-old
cobble stone beneath your hungering feet
make your legs mine

young student the sun shines across your forehead
I can not take this from you

your worldly accounts I keep like rich cocoa
a slow melting coffee bean coats the inside of my mouth

remember that slow night after the pub?
here in the States?

I led you to my bed then
the damask slid over our bodies creating us silk
thank you Egyptian cotton and excited linen
thank you crooning song and foolish wine
thank you dizzy moon
thank you drink and food and grape
Dionysus you are benevolent

thank you life
for what you gave when you gave it
I needed it then
we shared as the peacocks do
flashing our bright-eyed feathers
swaying sheer silk between the royal columns
I fluttered about like a nervous Leda and
you bent your neck like the swan

III.

sweet boy, I must rise now
this cow-heavy body is required
to meet the morning chore
my child cries out for me and I
am a modern woman
through and through
Amazon, I am
I rise with the sun like a farmer
carry baskets of fish and bread atop my head
I run like the Mayan mother
flaming torch and upside down child
duty calls

my child
split from the pain
and that long-ago
other man

IV.

(rationality sets in)
I must turn the sheets and finish the laundry now
drink the coffee and be the poet
I must live out divorcee as best I can

I best go tend to
the ever-present light bill
as the mailman has already
come and gone

forgive the mundane
for we know what we do

as you strap your feathered sandals
buckle shiny shoes around young heel
remember to pay me with a pile of coins

leave me this
gold and silver
leave it there upon
my stolid dark, wood
bedside table

a small visit in the mind's eye
give me only that

(please)

next time you touch Lorca
next time you brunch with Neruda
next time you dine in Morocco
from bowl to right hand to mouth and young hungry lip

next time you trample about,
big sandaled feet and open palm against
the big globe I always wished I knew

next time

think of me as I fold the
laundry and bare my breast
my child is hungry again
for I am stolid and will always bear fruit
for her

V.

you were too soon for me.
I have not yet molted
(please think of me)

I Would Love Like This If I Were You

If I were a man I would be dashing
not unlike the silver tip of sword
and the black cloak of Zorro, I
the mustachioed lip of hero and swooning love

If I were a man I'd whisper silvery minnows
that darted like intimate whispers
into your naked coiled ear of cupped flesh
silver flashes of true light
I'd waste away in your breath
and sweet feminine sweat
I'd gulp your musk from a greedy goblet
I would be the suicidal Romeo of your reverie

If I were a man I would be the
woman you always wanted me to be
the silence that only the trees can bring
when there is no wind to speak of

I would cup you like a womb and
be the barefoot male divinity
that of brute arm and dark hair
thick pelvis and broad waist
ripened shoulder and indestructible Achilles

I would take my cloak and
cover your nakedness
swashbuckle my way
into your memory

I'd be Bogart without the ego
Orson Welles without the selfishness

I would color your world
with all of the creative
energy I could muster

If I were a man I'd be
debonair and strike your fancy
the Laurence Olivier of glittering
desert and silk tents
yellow flapping yards of fabric
curling around the breeze
curling around the dry sun
that festoons your desolate sky

I would tiptoe around your clouds
offer my sinuous desire and motherly love
I would smooth the wrinkles
from your sad coat

I am no Diego
I would paint no one but you
jealous and guarded of your russet form

If I were your man
I'd bow my lovely head
like the soft brow of a velvety doe
I would surrender beneath the fern

Listen to me coo for you
like a flock of doves
like the spent rain
over summer mountains

I'd rent a thousand knives
of poetry into your quintessence
sweep over the Mojave as rain does

I would sprout for you,
the unexpected green life
from the parched cracked lip of dirt

If I were a man
I would clasp you to me
save myself in a silver locket
that breathes against your clavicle
and lay like soft metal against
the skin over your lungs
the copper taste of kisses
beneath the tongue

I'd be your burnt penny
I will be your Lorca

I would be the heart and safe sword
that held you like I would want to hold myself

If I were a man I would be dashing

The Don Quixote
of your afternoon poem
frail skinny old man with
the heart of a golden lion

I would trip over you like a windmill
paint you like a Spanish cubist
juxtapose your breasts against
the oil paint of strange angle
the awkward beauty of shape and sharp lines

drink me like watermelon
ample flesh and emerald rind
the ruby fruit fashioned from the
lovely garden of the aged contented wife

Drink me like a garden

I will not elude you
I will toil within you
I will be dashing through and through

This Sunday Morning

I like the honesty
in the swelling of
the skin when you
reach out for my clit

spoon dagger your four-
fingers around the column
of my thigh as I push
my small mango ass
against your body curled
around my body

Sunday morning – the light
has its way with us
burrowing and peeling
back our eyelids

I like the honesty
in your tongue,
as direct as a man's
starched work shirt
silken as pearlescent buttons
when you go down

Your ivory pink-tinged hands
part my brown thighs
as I sigh into the pillow
into the pulpit of me,
you speak truth
as true as the taste of
cold fruit on a hot tongue –
Guava

Last Thanksgiving
my father rejected you
So, I rejected him and we fled
that upside-down desert town

You were too white,
blonde butter cream curls,
eyes that burn as blue as
the strip of sky that followed
my car as we drove
the hell out of there

we picked our way
to your hometown to break
bread with your people

The dark beauty and
brutality of the South,
her history still
sweats memories of
plantation houseboys and mammies,
the legacy of dark water negligence
in the sorrow songs of Katrina,

where some people
still count on their fingers
how many nigger jokes
they can remember

We drove 15 hours to Shreveport,
Lousiana, stopping to fuck once
on the side of the highway
The diesel engines burned
down the world around us

We had our own thanks
to give – our bodies, mine,

brown as sand, simple as dirt
yours – not quite white, no
peach in places, burnt sunset
right before you turn salmon pink,
blood orange

The star inside of me
unraveled and I came
all over you and the passenger
seat of my car

Together, you and I
are a moveable feast

Kiwi – the grape on the vine,
toes, mouth, anus, pubis,
clavicle, the scent of *nopales*
and fresh mayhaw jam,
the smashing of bones, the
bodies' oils, the crest
of desire   rearing   pulling
small tidal waves in my chest
and out of my mouth

This Sunday morning
you push your way
into my cunt
and I let you.

We fuck away the
history of ignorance
the belt across my back,
the memory of your father's
fingers closing around
your throat cutting off
your power because
you spoke your mind
once or twice.

We fuck away all
those white boy jokes
my family insists
are funny

In the hollowed church
of our bed, our shared
Sundays are holy
There are no words
only orchestral moans
and darting tongues
we push our worlds into
one another – Baptist sermons
filled with brimstone and
the blood of a Catholic Christ.

We breathe life into
each others' lungs

Grapefuit – slivers of nectarine,
a rooted flower in the belly,
magnolia and sage, clit
tip of dick, so soft
hip bone on hip bone,
nipple to nipple, palms
bursting with *sangre de sandia,*
espiritu santo

Together we make
our own religion

I let you spoon dagger
your four fingers into
my mouth, this
is what we taste like,
like re-written history
like milk
like cinnamon

like sweet, sweet revolution
like slow, slow Sunday mornings.

I like the honesty
in the swelling
of this skin.

The Room Upstairs

It is a lonely bottle night
me and my cigarettes
my dogs
the smoke chokes the carpet
in her bed
our daughter is sleeping
like you do
all underwear
and no blanket
you curled up a
man-sized fetus on the couch
it is a declaration of your independence
I wish you were here
I am glad you are not
you strangle me
even in your sleep
even from downstairs
me in my safe haven on the second floor
divided by fourteen steps
and all of the world

our unspoken guilt
our brilliant arrogance

The empty stairwell tells of our separation
this mini divorce
we marry
we cleave
I gave birth to you
but you are not my child
and we know not the
pact of unconditional love

maybe by Wednesday
we will meet again

until then
I am proud Cuba
and you a stubborn embargo

the expanse of the Atlantic Ocean
is made of fourteen steps
twenty cigarettes
and two bottles of lonely
lukewarm beer

Ordinary Woman,
the Jilted Soapbox
or a List of Sorts

I who have left behind
trumpeting earrings, stashes of
tampons and empty bottle cap eyes,
scratched glasses and such
upon your night table,
lipstick in the shade of me and
my type of poetry all over your sheets.

All that I have left
behind I still carry
like a crooked spine, bruised
bag lady blues,
a spinster,

with all that nonsense
you squeezed from me
in those on-the-fly
psychoanalysis
late-night sessions,

the ones I first rejected
until I became accustomed
to speaking in your language

What now shall
I do with all these
ink blots and black ants?

You will clean your
man-house and soap
the dishes, the water will
glisten to the tops of
your forearms,

those hands that
made me feel so safe

You will unclog my
hair from your shower
and all the breath of me
will leave the room in
one long exhalation

the vanity mirror will have no
recollection that I was there

I, who have left behind a rainforest
of tears in your house, warmed
myself against your bonfires

let my little daughter
idle in the loft
for just a chance
that she should practice
with me
the embrace
I always
wanted her
to give you

Left behind,
my fleet of coffee mugs,
my faux-fur knee-high boots,
assorted panties and a silver
necklace that dangles from
the medicine cabinet

No books I'm sure,
I always read yours

There are last summer's
popsicles in your freezer
that you should throw out

Here is what
I have done
with your instructions,
rebellious to the bitter end.
You sent me away and
told me to draft a list
of my needs but all
I could think up
was this

a poem

how very
very
ordinary
of
me

These the Women
(or the Bruja Lament)

One little witch held love in a black crystal
she renounced all things smooth
pockets heavy with jaded bits of glass
a toilet bowl full of bile
hers was the story of matrimony

One little witch held love like light
a prism igniting in the combustible air of hope
she sailed a boat made of glass and faith
her smile like a child and roaring vivid
hers was the story of watercolor and morning

One little witch had eyes of a fox
cautious slivered stares and jerky twitch of neck
she fled like a doe
scattered quick like dead leaves in the wind
hers was the story of mistrust and belt buckle

One little witch hurled like a hurricane of fury
the wrath of furious fist and carnage
she left bloated bodies in her wake
ripped trees from root
left sailboats gutted on beach
hers was the story of tragic comedy and revenge

One little witch fused like hermaphrodite
metal melting and sex organ amalgamated
her mouth an open vacuum and vortex of famine
her mouth too much for the everyday man
hers was the story of hunger and wantonness

One little witch pushed her insides out
thighs streaked of blood like shooting star
the warm ulcer of womb suckled
chapped breast and chafe of porcelain-thin skin
her milk rose to a slow boil of cumbersome love
hers was the story of duplicity and motherhood

All had died a multitude of deaths
all were orchids bloody bruised and sweet like plums
all were vain and brilliant in their beauty
all had stroked the forehead of guilt
all held close incantations of unmet expectation
all acquiesced under burdensome boughs
heavy with blue snow
thick with all things meaty

All had tumbled
only to again erect

Again
the all of them
stewed in the sugary sweat
of open pore
boiled blood
black as tar
the chunk of placenta

Feathered
ancient
lonely in their godliness

The umbilical knows
no other way

On the Eve of My Abortion

there is a loudness
that fills me with silence
a blanket of white-sound
a roaring storm the size of a pinprick
muted lips, lashless eyes
I hold my breath
at the telling of this taboo

on the eve of my abortion
I become a woman of stone
who spouts tears of stone
and is insular in her sadness

I write one and then two
poems, birthing ideas
recreating me in the image
of the written word,
pulling a rib from thin air

on the eve of such a day
I am closeted, a secret thing
buried beneath a pile of clothes
I do not feel the fabric against my skin
I must become sinless
though I know there is no such
thing as sin

I have not bled in weeks
and I never knew I could
miss with such an aching
need that thing I often bemoan,
the stigmata of femininity

Today I ate a simple lunch
at a simple diner while
making pleasant conversation

the waitress, young and vital
her eyes were old and rimmed with worry

she spoke with a smile

the daily special,
the tepid soup
the niceties –
that Spring had finally,
finally arrived

I wondered if she had ever
done what I was about to do
and bit down the urge
to ask her, plain-spoken and
woman-to-woman

the blood bloomed
 to top of my tongue and
and the words were
silent thorns in my mouth
she moved on

I sat with my skin
until the
sun went down

on the night before my abortion
I am made of two bodies
a fractured arm like a white wing,
a black swan, glossy and swimming
inside the pool of myself

I can feel the blood
pumping through the lace and lattice,
the visceral veins, primordial
the way I was intended to be

On the eve of my abortion
it is raining inside of me
there is a great cloud
moving above the reflection
of a placid lake

I am a basin
about to fill
over

something sighs and breaks
but it isn't me

the size of a thumbnail
shifts like a fault line

all of my mother's saints
call out to me this evening
a bitter twilight martyred by the sun

Santa Teresa, the blessed venerable one
Our Virgin Mother, *virgincita morena*
Virgin de Guadalupe

I am still in my body
as a stampede of dark horses
run across the valley of my breasts,
creates the faintest ripple
of thunder

all the metaphors in the world
cannot save me from this poem

the office will be a blinding white,
the sheets spotlessly clean and my thighs
spread, cold at the touch of metal
this is not an offering, but a taking of –
the certitude of a mind made up
the resolution of my own verdict

I will maybe think of my other daughter
who sleeps now restfully in her bed,
one arm curled beneath her like a small wing,

I will maybe think of the waitress who
seemed to burst with newness
at the thought of Spring's arrival,

I will maybe think of the poems
I build one brick at a time,
the wistful need to bare fruit

still dogged,
decisions run
through my veins

thick as ice

Billie's Blues Are Mine

My gardenia scented getaway
suicide not for fame
dulling color fades today

I'm no Sylvia Plath mama,
sexy Anne Sexton, tragic Ophelia
won't go out mad martyr style
but sometimes the slide of
silky fingers collide with my sensibilities
sing a song of the lovely siren
that is the Lady

The smoky sad jazz
of Billie beckons me
blue deep, onyx sea
palette watery grave,
my gardenia-scented getaway

The greasy trombone
melodic boom of bass
guitar, light fingers
play piano keys,
tap in Morse code
the misery
through music,
honey butter songstress,
the bleeding heart
of Billie's mantra
my gardenia-scented homegirl

Sheets cover the windows
keeps the room cool and dark
when La Catrina speaks

bleached bone and bourgeois,

her skeletal thin-skinned
hand soothes me.
she hums death dreams,
lulls me to sleep,
smooth jazz reprieve

Silky fingers of subjugation
offer rest from the rage
that burns the heart, chatters
away my brain, thumps
my sleep out from
its groove, the
xylophone of my rib cage,
cradle to the downcast heart,
Silly moon.

So many odes
to that old girl
have they made,
Ms. Holiday, a good-
morning to heartache,
in her solitude going bad,
singing away
like no one can,
my sickness of sadness

You Frida lady,
Lady Lazarus,
Supernova woman
posturing pain
whispering,

muerto
   muerto
      muero

Llorona leave me be
prayers allow me to
channel la *chola loca*,
putita bruja
high hair,
devil-may-care
barrio bitch.

Something is passing
through these veins again
haunting my heart.
hopelessly hypnotic
a Homeric epic, needing release
heroin overdose all dressed
up and nowhere to go
needling straight to
the cardiac arrest,
slipping the noose around
the songbird's neck,
snap shut the nightingale
who will sing less and
less and less

knowing this day will come again,
and I will do as Dylan says and
Rage, rage, rage against the
dying of the light

And only if,
how I wish,
wonder if,
his villanelle
encompasses
the ladies too

and not just
the deaths of
fathers and old men

Tomorrow is a Zach de la Rocha day,
Charles Bukowski, Diane Wakowski,
A *pinche puta* Cisneros day.

Tomorrow will be
walk on Washington,
bulldog-battle along the border,
a fight for the brown

but today I sit
in the lovely gray,
the cleansing rain,
of Lady Day

Beauty

Beauty, I can't promise
you much but the hard
kind of love made soft
by my own pair of hands –
the splitting of my thighs
like the cleft of nectarine
and the muted blood of motherhood

the early morning of your birth
colored the sky a certain shade of rose
I will never see again
and I labored the whole night away
like a lone train in the dark

the months you spent inside of me
crafted a name – *Mia, Mine*

you were a river that spilled from within,
born praising Spring you split the air with your cries
my body bled announcing your arrival –
a dark ribbon inside of me, unfolding

yielding
to your soft coiled body,
and my skin was alive with you

your father shed his ego
on the day you were born and I never
saw him so naked and pure

I should have known then
we were a bit too possessive,
calculative, mechanical things
the way good parents can be,
the way we change,

the way the tendrils of our scars wrap
around the ankles of our children

Beauty, this was years before
I became enamored with the
fanfare of divorce, before we
spoke through lawyers and angry-lipped
phone calls

before we lost
track of you, our mangled
voices seeping into the walls of
your sleeping bedroom

our bent voices
brutal to your ears
red sickle-shaped words
we hurled at one another

how we suffer our little children
with our flint-rock tongues,
how we split hairs over money,
the cold bread of the dead

I blame him
for that knife in the back
he brought to our bed,
my shameless groveling
the secret closet where he
choked me
while I was nine months
swollen with you

I blame me
all those wrap-around thoughts
only a manic depressive knows
for my bitter tongue, my acidic love
the dumb pretty
poems I wrote

in the shadow of this sadness
I remember the small pale face of my mother,
the red threats my father's mouth made –
their desperate and clumsy attempts towards happiness

Beauty, forgive us
we were rough-hearted, children-turned-parents
young once and in love with the world,
we became old so fast –
ten shades of grey we fell
tumbling and tangled

You were conceived in the bluster of a winter desert
sand in our eyes, we were two bull-headed lovers
who groped for one another in the darkness

we held you
so we wouldn't have to hold
onto our own shapeless loneliness

but this is how we get by, right?
on a morsel of regret and what we
think we know of love –

this is how
we say
we are
sorry

us

Tell me about the lazy days
and I will recollect summer
nights like a basket full of
yarn tattered strings blowing
in the wind, colorless
Mama's cotton
linen on the line, the moon like
a basketball in the sky

before the idea of college
the smell of success
and mother's spilled milk,
her midnight attempt
with a razor meant for
shaving her eyebrows

We were thin-skinned kids
tongues a perpetual red
from the choke-cherry slurpees
we washed down our gullets and
a pocket full of stolen Slim-Jims
from the corner store

We always had a get-away plan
young criminals that we were
the Korean manager,
just as cliché
as us

all those times
we spat
in the wind

The desert had yet to set
us in our ways
the sun a golden pocket
watch on the other side of the globe

I saw it sink
between the handlebars
of my second-hand blue
beach cruiser each lazy warm
afternoon we spent together

A town with too
many rich ranchers
and not enough rivers
these were those days
before we baked into the
gingerbread figurines we became
knees still malleable, flexible
and young for good tree climbing
a tussle with our current bitch
mutt-dog in our dirt-packed back yard

Your smile was not yet shattered
my ribcage still intact our
breath held in traction
taken hostage by the stars
a whole desert just for us

We led miniature riots in our backyard
complete with wonder and the notion
that we could dig our way to China

dirt-filled nostrils our shared bathwater
was black as earth, two grubby-eyed kids
sharing the same soap

Brother, my little raven-haired dove
your bangs fell like crooked curtains

around the brow of your face
forever a lippy pout, a puckered
old man's question mark

You loved me then
not the way you
hate me now
and I always cried
when our father
hit you

but my hands
were just
as red as his
heart-heavy
as any guilt

I cried when at the age of nineteen
you smoked thirteen bowls of hashish
proud you didn't puke
smack went your newly
razor-bladed baldness
against my sliding window,
the pane shattered and
your lazy left eye rolled too crazy for me
as you limped away
I knew a part of you
was gone for good

sometimes you call
sometimes you won't
often I push you
many times
I don't
but when
you do
call

I hear those shattered
stars in your voice
and I know
the memory
of desert
has had
her salt-rubbed way
with us

Chloe

when no one answers your phone calls,
when the rain is dripping on the pitched roof of your home
when you can't stand one more thought about the absence
they are all sleeping
the way your daughter does in her bed now
and what is left of your ragged breathing
is a poem you may never write

I wonder if that is what happened to her
my friend alone in the crypt of her apartment
saying good night to the moon, blowing out the last candle
    on her night stand
did she hum softly to a Celtic drum?
did her hair cascade across her bare shoulders, the milky white
    of her neck
what last bone broke inside of her?
was it the rib?
was it the third phone call that fell on deaf ears?
how did she stumble into this fate?

I have dreamt her solace before
held it close like a numb knife to my neck
imagined I might
in the shower
the closet
alone in the cushion of my bed
lick the salt of loneliness
and curl around my shoulder blades
one last heaving time

men will walk away from this perfect sadness
leave their unused boxes in the corner of a room
dust in the shape of a coffin where his favorite couch stood
now removed, a letter like a bomb on the kitchen table

for a mother and her little daughter to grope at, wipe
confused cheeks against their tears –
how they glimmer

this is a summer of loss, cruel sunshine illuminates
every perceptible corner of your grief

we cannot hide from it
we must stare into eyes like mannequins
and realize they are our own

we will sing a dirty limerick
a drunken brawl song and wail away the dead
we will burn this house
say goodnight moon
spit the smoke from our mouths
and crush the last cigarette
with our bare feet

the poets will have their say,
they will

inhale the pain

and a brief candle
will exhale
for good

Cool Woman Albuquerque

Cool Woman Albuquerque is a city of many words
heaps of rags and scarves and hands that smell of oil
she is a bag lady.
she is a homeless city
her shoulders are made of watermelon rock and smooth silt
thin veins once a roaring river now muddied and pungent with stick
    and debris
her pockets are heavy with laundry mats and neon light
her pockets are heavy with beggars and banks and midnight pubs
hookah lounges
tattoo parlors
prostitutes prowl her sidewalks and boys call her dirty names
she has a certain gratitude for misplaced shopping carts and
    musicians
she has a certain gratitude for sloppy graffiti and cholo-hobo effigies

Her hot mouth houses roasting chile
roja, the flame of a summer Bosque
wild, roaring and in love with abandonment
stray dogs limp along her one-way streets
she is flea bitten and tangled all the way from Nob Hill to
    Downtown Friday night
she welcomes transplants and refugees and the rich balloonist
her hands are callused and reach feeble for spare change
squatting in the park
she takes a piss
lovers kiss
in her dark alleys and
the secret parts of her parks
the secret homes of the homeless

She is a water color dawn
a jackpot mad jangle of Indian Casino

she a dreadlocked hippie and a crystal meth-junkie
a mall rat, a college professor
a dusty book store prowler
a second-hand Goodwill shopping spree

Cool Woman Albuquerque spreads her legs
dips her turquoise topped toes into
the four corners of the sacred wind
and smiles for the photographer

she hangs lewd and naked in Santa Fe museums
highway billboards
the glossy pages of a turista magazine
her ass is branded with a stolen Zia
streaked in gold and waving
like a dumb child from a flag pole
Ristra braided hair
neck of honey
ankles thick like masa

She speaks in tongues
Diné
Spanglish
slang and catcalls

broken English and
open mic-night poetry
that makes no sense

her underbelly of avenues
house abortion clinics
hidden Buddhist temples and pool halls
free lunch lines in Central Park

upon her breast wild flocks of pigeons roam
like college kids drunk on freedom

her thoughts are peppered with clouds of cotton
her bones ancient as dust
her lungs engraved in streams of silver

She daydreams
of parades and *quinceañeras*
her ears ring
of cathedrals gone mad
the clanging belfry of morning mass
the clamor of feast day upon a sunny dusty reservation

Her shawl is stitched in stories
her tattered slippers patched in words.
her tousled hair tangled in early morning traffic jams

She is the history of today
a filthy mosaic of gutters and a flooded out Barrelas.
the front page of the defunct Tribune

Cool Woman Albuquerque is a bag
lady with a broken back
a smile like the missing teeth
of an old picket fence

She is a cherry red ranfla cruising Route 66!

Beautiful! Glorious!
Orale!

A city riddled in the jagged splendor of mountain chain
upon mountain chain
upon the pink salmon hue of a
golden
radiant
mountain chain.

Cool Woman Albuquerque
is a man
of many words.

My Aging Face

My aging face is like the moon
craters and pock marks gone amuck
moon shoe footprints stamp their
exploration all over my laugh lines

I revel in the newness of my oldness
that I suspect in the mirror
I watch how crow's
feet mosh in a collective
concerto, cliff dive off
the razor sharp Jemez
of my cheekbones
wrinkles will do
the backstroke into
the pools of skin
skinny-dipping under
each squinted eye

I dry
like baked sand
red clay
evaporated
water

I wouldn't exchange this skin
for any other, no other skin
could tell my story
sing a psalm for mothers
my arms shape a cradle
my skin spoons my lover
no other skin can spell
the havoc and strife,
the strain of stretch marks,
the clumsy cesarean scar mark,

the way the rolling landscape of my belly can
the way the slow descent of the valley of the breasts can
the Panama Canal split of skin can
the gorge of discolored puckered skin can
no other skin can tell my story like it can

I want time to ravage my face
roughen my cheeks like the
ruins of Macchu Picchu
I want my eyebrows to grow out into
a single bird,
like the one that flies
the face that frames Frida

I want Plato to play about
my drooping chin
dropping in to carve
out the deepest of manifestos
a map of Hellenic proportions

I want gravity to play
croquette upon my forehead
stop for tea around my two lips
and spill its wrinkled secrets
bleeding the edges of my lipstic
pursing the peck of all my kisses

Time do what you will
to my body, play savage
chords upon my biology
ripen my theology
feed my voracious hunger for poetry
insatiable poetry
kissing poetry
drinking poetry
licking poetry

color divinity
upon the tops
of my hands and
between my legs
grey my hair
down there
until I see
God

the dark star
of menopause
Autumn of my ovaries
Indian Summer
Winter slumber
silly solstice of the womb

Years of knotting my daughter's braids and buns
fixing up buttons, tying shoes and typing memories
will have tangled the joints of fingers, disjointed discs
worn out wombs, curving
a spine like a smile
hunching an old lady
into happiness

My aging face is like Port
the long wait of faith
a goblet of ripened wine
a porous cork and
a dying of blush in the cheeks

Surely

Surely I can hold onto this delicious Sunday
arch and curl my back into the patch of sunlight
streaked with clarity and sobriety across my bed.

Breaking the barrier of such dirty windows,
grey with misgivings is a full day's work.

The dog lies languid atop my head breathing
hot air into my ears as, panty-clad,
I hunch over my poetry and sip at my tepid soup.

Sunday is seen without
the veil of finely netted
misgivings, red-veins popping
at the corner of glassy eyes.
The kohl-rimmed guilt
of late-night transgressions
does not fetter the mind.

When you consider
what I have left behind
this Sunday does not
seem so meandering
compared to the usual
reverie of madness.

I have been busy
Ignoring the corner of ashy pubs
the crooked steps back to the car
the fumbling of foil rubber wrapper

Last night, somewhere, there is
a bar room of ghost pirates

chains clatter and pints still
swill like the madness of marauders.
Barstools clank and smash over heads,
in some dirty bathroom mirror
the women wink their red-hot
cigarette eyes into their
reflections of nothingness,
spend fast money or
the money of fast men.

The night is wicked
fast on my trail
waiting for Sunday
to wreak its havoc,
The barrage of reprisal
banging at my head –
The strange man-shaped
lump at the side of my bed,
groans and shifts the stink of
his weight towards me

Clattering, the night haunts my
day and faintly I see through the
bottom of a foggy beer mug the
skinless ghosts and lipless smiles,
shiny teeth polished to the bone

These new Sundays are
delicious and precarious
guarded, tentatively instead
I take up with the dog

Deliriously happy he is,
my new little husband
I have been gone a long time,
my dear hearted one

Without wine or spirit
but with a fearful welcome
of such a fine, upstanding
Sunday morning.

The last remnants of peace
my last fragmented chance.

Una Carta de Amor de la Llorona
with special thanks to Danny Solis

open a jar for the dead, the winds of an open-
mouthed river like a fishy kiss, oily, will ride up your neck
it has been minutes, decades only a day since
the departure of my cherub stones, my children
made of pitfalls and marble, two pairs
of trusting eyes

the moon a witness to their slipping away
beneath a blackness like the spit of a serpent,
the river who froths at her lipless mouth

I am a wandering offrenda, a
burning white flame, a woman
without footprints

Ay, diablo! pull my fantastic hair of colorless ribbon,
shred me with your long talons like *papel picado*
like eyelets of a delicate dirty lace
you are my inverted love, my mariachi monstrosity
pull me into the dirt with you,
I will rub this sand between my legs, haunches ragged
with the smell of your open palm
you are the closest thing to a man

let your onion eyes linger
over my crow eaten bones
you are the living thing inside
of my dead moon,
the noose of my womb,
the worm-rotten entrails

pine away, you silver-footed devil, tongue of a bastard,
I have seen a meandering love like yours before,

now my lidless eyes are peeled back over my skull as I watch
you with all of the blood and wrath I have ever known
I spit on your pile of ash, your pious truth, your pitiful love

I have no use for the stone hearts of men
or the monsters who used to be men

What shame my husband brought to us,
you should have seen his lackluster eyes,
his ghostly slit that spoke to the back of my head
his pockets empty with gold, head full of stale air
his arrogant thighs
his high-cropped riding pants
his slick stallion
like bitter potatoes he cast us back to the earth

When he paraded that woman,
made of silk and parasol,
hot coals scorched my eyes
my peasant knuckles yearned for
something to smash against

I am a love-shorn bride,
a barefoot gaggle of ball and socket
take this piece of hip-bone
carve it into an obsidian blade and
cut this womb from me. *Ay,*
Cucui torture me soft with your
light-footed rooster, madman dance
acid rain letters of the dead

we will fashion a house of sticks and burnt stone,
cobbled brick of blackened bread
the windows shades made of our eyelids
sightless so that I might not remember
the spectacle of the river

you will let me forget I ever gave birth
and instead I will forge you from the jelly of my gut

Ay, El Muerto, you knock-kneed skeleton
you are the husband I am meant to have
our beloved bridal bed wilts like
white magnolia and softens like curdled milk

Tell me, dark lord, in whose
child shall I find reprieve?
What thin-ankled dark-haired
beauty will become my savior,
my temporary resurrection?

I am no Medusa –
I will ink out these stars,
stick a dagger in every last one of them.
I will blind the night.
I am all that whispers, the knotted hair of Hemlock,
a banshee, misfit cry,
a bag full of misbegotten keys,
the sour breath of grief

I tend my garden of stewed tomato
and maggoty meat, a bushel of eyelashes
and children's smiles
my gardens are overgrown
with thickets, with the laces of
tiny shoes, bits of colored foil,
pin-wheels and yarn,
the tattered love of a mother

Two Weeks Into the Break

I have become courageous with my solemnity
face like a dried peach pit, the set jaw I show
off in the brackish noisy public I have come to disdain
like a vampire shopping for milk, eyes like red-rimmed lasers
gut-wrenching cramps from unintentional fasts and snot rags
avalanche from the couch as I twist in my sleep –

I burn like a skinless fish on the frying pan
dance, little minnow, dance like the dead thing you are
I have acquired the bravado to become a true martyr
I crack my knuckles like peanut shells, I make non-
sequitor jokes at the television and cry when I masturbate
this poem isn't even funny
and I tried

two weeks into the break then fate said,
"Here's a healthy dose of menstrual cramps
a week earlier than you expected. Bleed mammal."
I cried when I saw the blood on my panties
it was about to get worse before it got worse

I am talented with this game of pyrotechnics
a close cousin to chaos, swimming with needles
burning sage like a cosmic hippie trying to
smoke away his figment of bad odor

two weeks into the break and I break
the lining of my uterus unfurling into another
reminder that I will never have his children
that you can't take back abortions

but nightwalkers don't carry wombs with them
only restless midnight grocery coupons, fangs
sharpened on another life they never lived,
the last body they sucked clean

they idle in the shampoo aisle, pay their
bills behind two-sizes too-big black sunglasses
a Jackie O. before she turned Marilyn
a Marilyn before she fell to sleep for always

the first week of break up is a serial killer
the second week is a post office shoot-up
the third a new abberation I will sink myself into,
next week proudly flashing my badge

waiting for the sun to burn me awake

I Dreamt of Possession

there is a shoebox with a gun it
a backbone without a home, a wet cat prowling at the door
mewing like a nervous prostitute
Boxcar, my pretty
lay down your roaming train tracks
stop moving through the rain
let me get my big 'ol needy hands around that slippery body of yours
that androgynous back and those soft velvety moles
the springcurl of your hair makes me wet inside,
a dozen melting candles drip down my thighs
a sopping mess of emotions pooling around my toes
at least I'm not bleeding tonight

I wished you hated me more than you do
but you cry like a child when you come into me
and I want to be battered like the wind
hate me so that I may love you
your pistol-whip blue eyes
hurt because they are too kind
and I need to press against a hot spoon
a bullet-riddled chest, a man with
a mangled past and a cowboy trick up his sleeve

my feminist rancor curled her lip
at the woman in my mirror
and I says, so I says,
to her –

you wouldn't know
love if it spit in your face

you don't
know nothin'
from a hole
in the ground

Santuario de Guadalupe

Santa Fe, New Mexico, est. 1795
oldest church and shrine dedicated to
Our Virgin Guadalupe

through a thick sky
heavy with the promise of regret
the flower stems bend
at their waist, green knees
snap between the fingers
of ink-stained boys, who are
men growing into their skin;
they have been old
their whole lives

the walls of the *santuario* quivers
at the approach of their
swaggering bravado
and the roses shudder
to think their end is nigh
I would like to hope
la Virgen has forgiven
their future transgressions

I shield them from nothing,
as their teacher, their mentor;
they ride their youth like
lightning. I herd them
like wild horses and they
stamp their hooves to create
thunder in the ground

for all of my goading,
and perpetual mothering
they reward me with slices
of their carnivorous smiles,
an army of lowered eyes

a moment of respect
it is all
I can hope for

these beautiful boys
who own their girls
who drive their
mothers to madness
roaming fatherless figures

And the girls – who
toss their hair like
nervous mares and
smile like the sun
that breaks apart
the regrettable sky

they receive their
offering like a
basket of gold

as if Samson himself
laid the length of his
hair across their feet

a head full of flaming
petals, decapitated –
a green torso cast
earthward soon to
become one with
the dirt again

the rooted body
of a marble saint
looks on but
says nothing
at such desecration,

her womb empty
for some time now –
a sonless mother

Run hard against
the wind I want
to cry out to
them – young women,
turn your backs on
such acts of love –
their hearts are
Thunderbird
the last drop of
wine from a
cheap plastic cup

you will shred your
slender fingers upon
their thorns

These boys want
to disown your body,
make a shallow grave of you

but even I can-
not look away
from their young
dark eyes

how they ripple
over the rose
garden
they shuffle their feet
extend their arms,
heads scuffing the
stone floor
dull tattoos claim

one street corner
or another

they gift death, the
stiff bodies of roses
alert in their palms,
bursting red blossoms
yellow tight buds
perfumed and pink
and weightless petals

the stems ooze
white milk from
their ripped-out necks

I receive their offering,
and take their roses
into me

My Mama Is a Poet

oh silly mama
why are you always scratching
words out of your head,
like nighttime pulgas, like old-school
rollers wrapped around the *pelos* of your bangs,
pink little pieces of crazy?

do you love poetry
more than me
or because of me?

oh silly mama
why you always muttering to yourself
switching your hips to and fro,
foaming up the dishes,
your narrow behind keeping time
bones clanking, elbows flapping
bumping to some unheard music
banging around
in that bellfry of a brain?

mama, will I be like you?
Like you, I say
will I be like you,
manless, big-footed and
loudmouthed?

Will men and mean-hearted women
stuff a dishtowel between my lips,
lock me in the basement, force me
to wash and fold their clothes?

Will I have to find the time to
rhyme between the chores?

Pretend I don't love my
poetry as much as I do,
fool myself into thinking I just
ain't that good?

oh silly silly mama,
will I ever forget to write?
will I ever learn to love
myself?

Why you always crying
sad sad mama?
hiding your tears
beneath the rainforest of a shower

If you want to forget
why you always
writing to remember?

Acknowledgments

There are many people to thank. First, *mil gracias* to my slam family of Albuquerque, a true grass roots group of empowered people changing the world for the better one poem at a time. Thank you Don McIver and Eric Bodwell, my slam poetry guardian angels. Thanks to my first mentor Merimee Moffit for her fiery feminist bad-assness and wisdom. Thank you to Levi Romero for his unwavering guidance and chicanismo. I still owe you a burger and beer, Levi. Of course, much gratitude for John Crawford of West End Press and for Lisa Gill and her expert eye as she combed through my manuscript. I will forever be indebted to my friend and photographer Gina Marselle. Thank you Zachary Kluckman for being my brother from another mother. Thank you Mariah B. for showing me what sisterhood really is. Much love to the Macondo Foundation and all of the lovely writers who have urged me to complete this book.

These poems could not have been written without the eternal love I have for my daughter, Mia "Sopapilla" Helena Rivera. I became a woman the day I gave birth to her. Thank you Mom, Dad, Pat and Angel for supporting and putting up with all my crazy slam poetry. And last. Not least. Thank you Buddha for your love.

—Jessica Helen Lopez